M000203522

From:

Date:

Message:

SERENITY PRAYER

Serenity Prayer

© 2016 Christian Art Gifts, RSA
        Christian Art Gifts Inc., IL, USA

First edition 2016

Designed by Christian Art Gifts

Images used under license from Shutterstock.com

Printed in China

ISBN 978-1-4321-1617-0

16 17 18 19 20 21 22 23 24 25 – 10 9 8 7 6 5 4 3 2 1

SERENITY PRAYER

God grant me the serenity
to accept the things I cannot change;
courage to change the things I can;
and wisdom to know the difference.

Living one day at a time;
enjoying one moment at a time;
accepting hardships as the pathway to peace;
taking, as He did, this sinful world
as it is, not as I would have it;
trusting that He will make all things right
if I surrender to His will;
that I may be reasonably happy in this life
and supremely happy with Him
forever in the next.
Amen.

Reinhold Niebuhr

Contents

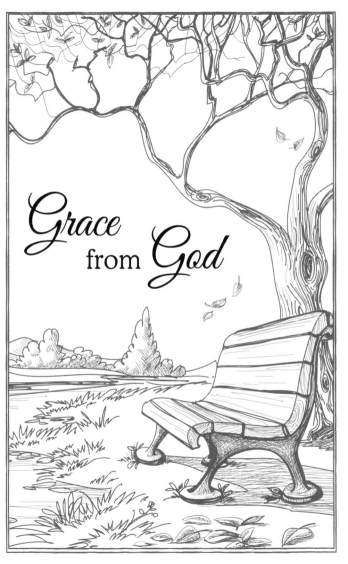

GRACE FROM GOD

For the LORD God is our sun and our shield.
He gives us grace and glory. The LORD will
withhold no good thing from those who do
what is right.

Psalm 84:11 NLT

With minds that are alert and fully sober, set
your hope on the grace to be brought to you
when Jesus Christ is revealed at His coming.

1 Peter 1:13 NIV

Rend your heart, and not your garments;
return to the LORD your God, for He is
gracious and merciful, slow to anger, and
of great kindness; and He relents from
doing harm.

Joel 2:13 NKJV

GRACE FROM GOD

To each one of us grace has been given as Christ apportioned it.

Ephesians 4:7 NIV

"My grace is sufficient for you, for My power is made perfect in weakness." Therefore I will boast all the more gladly of my weaknesses, so that the power of Christ may rest upon me. For the sake of Christ, then, I am content with weaknesses, insults, hardships, persecutions, and calamities. For when I am weak, then I am strong.

2 Corinthians 12:9-10 ESV

In Him we have redemption through His blood, the forgiveness of sins, according to the riches of His grace.

Ephesians 1:7 NKJV

GRACE FROM GOD

God saved you by His grace when you believed.
And you can't take credit for this; it is a gift
from God.

Ephesians 2:8 NLT

God is able to make all grace abound to you,
so that having all sufficiency in all things at all
times, you may abound in every good work.

2 Corinthians 9:8 ESV

Sin is no longer your master, for you no longer
live under the requirements of the law. Instead,
you live under the freedom of God's grace.

Romans 6:14 NLT

GRACE FROM GOD

Let us then approach God's throne of grace with confidence, so that we may receive mercy and find grace to help us in our time of need.

Hebrews 4:16 NIV

From His abundance we have all received one gracious blessing after another.

John 1:16 NLT

The LORD is compassionate and gracious, slow to anger, abounding in love.

Psalm 103:8 NIV

We praise God for the glorious grace He has poured out on us who belong to His dear Son.

Ephesians 1:6 NLT

GRACE FROM GOD

We are all saved the same way, by the undeserved grace of the Lord Jesus.

Acts 15:11 NLT

For the grace of God has appeared, bringing salvation for all people, training us to renounce ungodliness and worldly passions, and to live self-controlled, upright, and godly lives in the present age.

Titus 2:11-12 ESV

You know the generous grace of our Lord Jesus Christ. Though He was rich, yet for your sakes He became poor, so that by His poverty He could make you rich.

2 Corinthians 8:9 NLT

May our Lord Jesus Christ Himself and God our Father, who loved us and by His grace gave us eternal encouragement and good hope, encourage your hearts and strengthen you in every good deed and word.

2 Thessalonians 2:16-17 NIV

May you experience the love of Christ, though it is too great to understand fully. Then you will be made complete with all the fullness of life and power that comes from God.

Ephesians 3:19 NLT

Through Him we have also obtained access by faith into this grace in which we stand, and we rejoice in hope of the glory of God.

Romans 5:2 ESV

GRACE FROM GOD

Because of His grace He declared us righteous and gave us confidence that we will inherit eternal life.

Titus 3:7 NLT

The God of all grace, who called you to His eternal glory in Christ, after you have suffered a little while, will Himself restore you and make you strong, firm and steadfast.

1 Peter 5:10 NIV

Even before I was born, God chose me and called me by His marvelous grace.

Galatians 1:15 NLT

Finding
Contentment

FINDING CONTENTMENT

The righteous eat to their hearts' content, but the stomach of the wicked goes hungry.

Proverbs 13:25 NIV

True godliness with contentment is itself great wealth.

1 Timothy 6:6 NLT

We brought nothing into this world, and it is certain we can carry nothing out. And having food and clothing, with these we shall be content. But those who desire to be rich fall into temptation and a snare.

1 Timothy 6:7-9 NKJV

FINDING CONTENTMENT

Those who love money will never have enough. How meaningless to think that wealth brings true happiness! The more you have, the more people come to help you spend it. So what good is wealth – except perhaps to watch it slip through your fingers!

Ecclesiastes 5:10-11 NLT

The fear of the Lord leads to life; then one rests content, untouched by trouble.

Proverbs 19:23 NIV

Enjoy what you have rather than desiring what you don't have. Just dreaming about nice things is meaningless – like chasing the wind.

Ecclesiastes 6:9 NLT

FINDING CONTENTMENT

Keep your lives free from the love of money and be content with what you have, because God has said, "Never will I leave you; never will I forsake you."

Hebrews 13:5 NIV

"Beware! Guard against every kind of greed. Life is not measured by how much you own."

Luke 12:15 NLT

I have learned in whatever situation I am to be content. I know how to be brought low, and I know how to abound. In any and every circumstance, I have learned the secret of facing plenty and hunger, abundance and need.

Philippians 4:11-12 ESV

FINDING CONTENTMENT

I am content with weaknesses, insults,
hardships, persecutions, and calamities.
For when I am weak, then I am strong.

2 Corinthians 12:10 NLT

Remove falsehood and lies far from me;
give me neither poverty nor riches – feed
me with the food allotted to me; lest I be full
and deny You, and say, "Who is the LORD?"
Or lest I be poor and steal, and profane the
name of my God.

Proverbs 30:8-9 NKJV

The LORD is my shepherd; I shall not want. He
makes me lie down in green pastures. He leads
me beside still waters.

Psalm 23:1-2 ESV

Better to have little, with godliness, than to be rich and dishonest.

Proverbs 16:8 NLT

Command those who are rich in this present age not to be haughty, nor to trust in uncertain riches but in the living God, who gives us richly all things to enjoy. Let them do good, that they be rich in good works, ready to give, willing to share, storing up for themselves a good foundation for the time to come, that they may lay hold on eternal life.

1 Timothy 6:17-19 NKJV

The backslider in heart will be filled with the fruit of his ways, and a good man will be filled with the fruit of his ways.

Proverbs 14:14 ESV

FINDING CONTENTMENT

Better the little that the righteous have than the wealth of many wicked.

Psalm 37:16 NIV

A sound heart is life to the body, but envy is rottenness to the bones.

Proverbs 14:30 NKJV

Whatever my eyes desired I did not keep from them. I did not withhold my heart from any pleasure, for my heart rejoiced in all my labor; and this was my reward from all my labor. Then I looked on all the works that my hands had done and on the labor in which I had toiled; and indeed all was vanity and grasping for the wind. There was no profit under the sun.

Ecclesiastes 2:10-11 NKJV

"Don't store up treasures here on earth, where moths eat them and rust destroys them, and where thieves break in and steal. Store your treasures in heaven, where moths and rust cannot destroy, and thieves do not break in and steal. Wherever your treasure is, there the desires of your heart will also be."

Matthew 6:19-21 NLT

Make it your ambition to lead a quiet life: You should mind your own business and work with your hands, just as we told you, so that your daily life may win the respect of outsiders and so that you will not be dependent on anybody.

1 Thessalonians 4:11-12 NIV

A greedy man stirs up strife, but the one who trusts in the LORD will be enriched.

Proverbs 28:25 ESV

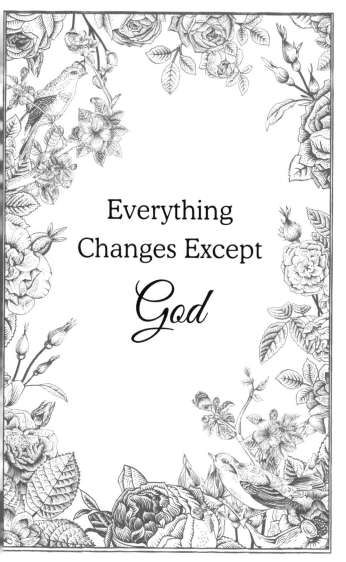

Everything
Changes Except
God

EVERYTHING CHANGES
EXCEPT GOD

Jesus Christ is the same yesterday and today and forever.

Hebrews 13:8 NIV

"For I am the LORD, I do not change; therefore you are not consumed."

Malachi 3:6 NKJV

LORD, You remain the same forever! Your throne continues from generation to generation.

Lamentations 5:19 NLT

The grass withers and the flowers fall, but the word of our God endures forever.

Isaiah 40:8 NIV

EVERYTHING CHANGES EXCEPT GOD

"You, Lord, laid the foundation of the earth in the beginning, and the heavens are the work of Your hands; they will perish, but You remain; they will all wear out like a garment, like a robe You will roll them up, like a garment they will be changed. But You are the same, and Your years will have no end."

Hebrews 1:10-12 ESV

God is not human, that He should lie, not a human being, that He should change His mind. Does He speak and then not act? Does He promise and not fulfill?

Numbers 23:19 NIV

"I am the Alpha and the Omega, the Beginning and the End, the First and the Last."

Revelation 22:13 NKJV

EVERYTHING CHANGES EXCEPT GOD

Whatever is good and perfect is a gift coming down to us from God our Father, who created all the lights in the heavens. He never changes or casts a shifting shadow.

James 1:17 NLT

Of old You laid the foundation of the earth, and the heavens are the work of Your hands. They will perish, but You will endure; yes, they will all grow old like a garment; like a cloak You will change them, and they will be changed. But You are the same, and Your years will have no end.

Psalm 102:25-27 NKJV

Have you not known? Have you not heard? The LORD is the everlasting God, the Creator of the ends of the earth.

Isaiah 40:28 ESV

EVERYTHING CHANGES
EXCEPT GOD

Your word, LORD, is eternal; it stands firm
in the heavens. Your faithfulness continues
through all generations; You established the
earth, and it endures. Your laws endure to this
day, for all things serve You.

Psalm 119:89-91 NIV

Lord, through all the generations You have
been our home! Before the mountains were
born, before You gave birth to the earth and the
world, from beginning to end, You are God.

Psalm 90:1-2 NLT

The plans of the LORD stand firm forever, the
purposes of His heart through all generations.

Psalm 33:11 NIV

EVERYTHING CHANGES EXCEPT GOD

Because God wanted to make the unchanging nature of His purpose very clear to the heirs of what was promised, He confirmed it with an oath. God did this so that, by two unchangeable things in which it is impossible for God to lie, we who have fled to take hold of the hope set before us may be greatly encouraged.

Hebrews 6:17-18 NIV

If we are unfaithful, He remains faithful, for He cannot deny who He is.

2 Timothy 2:13 NLT

He who is the Glory of Israel does not lie or change His mind; for He is not a human being, that He should change His mind.

1 Samuel 15:29 NIV

EVERYTHING CHANGES
EXCEPT GOD

They shall speak of the glory of Your kingdom and tell of Your power, to make known Your mighty deeds, and the glorious splendor of Your kingdom. Your kingdom is an everlasting kingdom, and Your dominion endures throughout all generations.

Psalm 145:11-13 ESV

"I alone am God! I am God, and there is none like Me. Only I can tell you the future before it even happens. Everything I plan will come to pass, for I do whatever I wish. I will call a swift bird of prey from the east – a leader from a distant land to come and do My bidding. I have said what I would do, and I will do it."

Isaiah 46:9-11 NLT

EVERYTHING CHANGES EXCEPT GOD

Give thanks to the LORD, for He is good. His love endures forever.

Psalm 136:1 NIV

Praise the LORD, the God of Israel, who lives from everlasting to everlasting.

Psalm 41:13 NLT

My days are like the evening shadow; I wither away like grass. But You, LORD, sit enthroned forever; Your renown endures through all generations.

Psalm 102:11-12 NIV

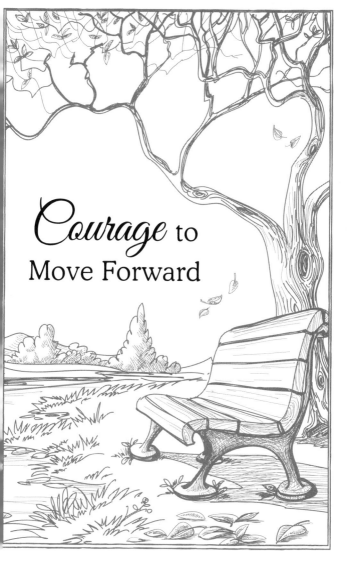

Courage to
Move Forward

COURAGE TO
MOVE FORWARD

"Fear not, for I am with you; be not dismayed, for I am your God. I will strengthen you, yes, I will help you, I will uphold you with My righteous right hand."

Isaiah 41:10 NKJV

Be strong and courageous. Do not be afraid; do not be discouraged, for the LORD your God will be with you wherever you go.

Joshua 1:9 NIV

Be strong and of good courage, do not fear nor be afraid of them; for the LORD your God, He is the One who goes with you. He will not leave you nor forsake you.

Deuteronomy 31:6 NKJV

COURAGE TO MOVE FORWARD

In Your strength I can crush an army; with my God I can scale any wall.

Psalm 18:29 NLT

The wicked flee when no one pursues, but the righteous are bold as a lion.

Proverbs 28:1 NKJV

Be strong and take heart, all you who hope in the LORD.

Psalm 31:24 NIV

In the day when I cried out, You answered me, and made me bold with strength in my soul.

Psalm 138:3 NKJV

COURAGE TO
MOVE FORWARD

Be strong in the LORD and in His mighty power.

Ephesians 6:10 NIV

If God is for us, who can ever be against us?

Romans 8:31 NLT

Surely the righteous will never be shaken; they will be remembered forever. They will have no fear of bad news; their hearts are steadfast, trusting in the LORD.

Psalm 112:6-7 NIV

Be on guard. Stand firm in the faith. Be courageous. Be strong.

1 Corinthians 16:13 NLT

COURAGE TO MOVE FORWARD

Therefore, my dear brothers and sisters, stand firm. Let nothing move you. Always give yourselves fully to the work of the Lord, because you know that your labor in the Lord is not in vain.

1 Corinthians 15:58 NIV

Yea, though I walk through the valley of the shadow of death, I will fear no evil; for You are with me; Your rod and Your staff, they comfort me.

Psalm 23:4 NKJV

When I am afraid, I put my trust in You. In God, whose word I praise, in God I trust; I shall not be afraid. What can flesh do to me?

Psalm 56:3-4 ESV

COURAGE TO MOVE FORWARD

Be of good courage, and let us be strong for our people and for the cities of our God. And may the LORD do what is good in His sight.

2 Samuel 10:12 NKJV

Jesus immediately said to them: "Take courage! It is I. Don't be afraid."

Matthew 14:27 NIV

Be strong and courageous and do it. Do not be afraid and do not be dismayed, for the LORD God, even my God, is with you. He will not leave you or forsake you.

1 Chronicles 28:20 ESV

COURAGE TO
MOVE FORWARD

Take courage! For I believe God. It will be just as He said.

Acts 27:25 NLT

When the angel of the LORD appeared to Gideon, he said, "The LORD is with you, mighty warrior."

Judges 6:12 NIV

You will prosper, if you take care to fulfill the statutes and judgments with which the LORD charged Moses concerning Israel. Be strong and of good courage; do not fear nor be dismayed.

1 Chronicles 22:13 NKJV

COURAGE TO
MOVE FORWARD

Do not be afraid. Stand firm and you will see
the deliverance the LORD will bring you today.
The LORD will fight for you; you need only to
be still.

Exodus 14:13-14 NIV

Be strong and courageous ... It is the LORD who
goes before you. He will be with you; He will
not leave you or forsake you. Do not fear or
be dismayed.

Deuteronomy 31:7-8 ESV

God has not given us a spirit of fear, but of
power and of love and of a sound mind.

2 Timothy 1:7 NKJV

God Gives Wisdom

Get wisdom, get understanding; do not forget my words or turn away from them. Do not forsake wisdom, and she will protect you; love her, and she will watch over you.

Proverbs 4:5-6 NIV

Your testimonies are wonderful; therefore my soul keeps them. The entrance of Your words gives light; it gives understanding to the simple.

Psalm 119:129-130 NKJV

"I will instruct you and teach you in the way you should go; I will counsel you with My loving eye on you."

Psalm 32:8 NIV

GOD GIVES WISDOM

Fear of the LORD is the foundation of true wisdom. All who obey His commandments will grow in wisdom.

Psalm 111:10 NLT

The wisdom that comes from heaven is first of all pure; then peace-loving, considerate, submissive, full of mercy and good fruit, impartial and sincere.

James 3:17 NIV

Wisdom is sweet to your soul. If you find it, you will have a bright future, and your hopes will not be cut short.

Proverbs 24:14 NLT

GOD GIVES WISDOM

If you call out for insight and cry aloud for understanding, and if you look for it as for silver and search for it as for hidden treasure, then you will understand the fear of the LORD and find the knowledge of God. For the LORD gives wisdom; from His mouth come knowledge and understanding.

Proverbs 2:3-6 NIV

If you need wisdom, ask our generous God, and He will give it to you. He will not rebuke you for asking.

James 1:5 NLT

How much better to get wisdom than gold, to get insight rather than silver!

Proverbs 16:16 NIV

GOD GIVES WISDOM

"I will give you the right words and such wisdom that none of your opponents will be able to reply or refute you!"

Luke 21:15 NLT

The law of the LORD is perfect, refreshing the soul. The statutes of the LORD are trustworthy, making wise the simple.

Psalm 19:7 NIV

We know that the Son of God has come, and He has given us understanding so that we can know the true God. And now we live in fellowship with the true God because we live in fellowship with His Son, Jesus Christ.

1 John 5:20 NLT

GOD GIVES WISDOM

To God belong wisdom and power; counsel and understanding are His.

Job 12:13 NIV

Listen to counsel and receive instruction, that you may be wise in your latter days.

Proverbs 19:20 NKJV

God gives wisdom, knowledge, and joy to those who please Him.

Ecclesiastes 2:26 NLT

By wisdom a house is built, and by understanding it is established; by knowledge the rooms are filled with all precious and pleasant riches.

Proverbs 24:3-4 ESV

GOD GIVES WISDOM

Praise the name of God forever and ever, for He has all wisdom and power. He gives wisdom to the wise and knowledge to the scholars.

Daniel 2:20-21 NLT

The wise shall inherit glory, but shame shall be the legacy of fools.

Proverbs 3:35 NKJV

Wisdom will multiply your days and add years to your life. If you become wise, you will be the one to benefit. If you scorn wisdom, you will be the one to suffer.

Proverbs 9:11-12 NLT

GOD GIVES WISDOM

The fear of the LORD is the beginning of wisdom, and knowledge of the Holy One is understanding.

Proverbs 9:10 NIV

Wisdom will enter your heart, and knowledge will fill you with joy. Wise choices will watch over you. Understanding will keep you safe. Wisdom will save you from evil people, from those whose words are twisted.

Proverbs 2:10-12 NLT

Instruct the wise and they will be wiser still; teach the righteous and they will add to their learning.

Proverbs 9:9 NIV

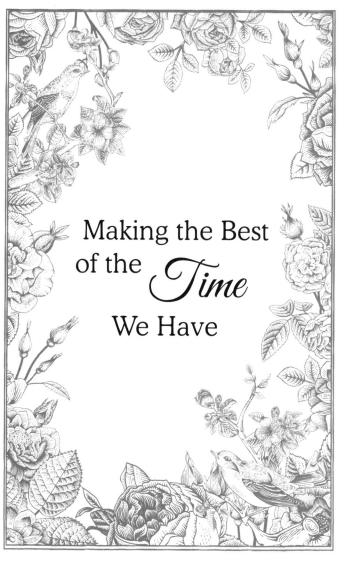

Making the Best of the *Time* We Have

MAKING THE BEST OF THE TIME WE HAVE

Be very careful, then, how you live – not as unwise but as wise, making the most of every opportunity, because the days are evil.

Ephesians 5:15-16 NIV

"We must quickly carry out the tasks assigned us by the One who sent us. The night is coming, and then no one can work. But while I am here in the world, I am the light of the world."

John 9:4-5 NLT

Teach us to number our days, that we may gain a heart of wisdom.

Psalm 90:12 NIV

MAKING THE BEST OF THE TIME WE HAVE

Since his days are determined, and the number of his months is with You, and You have appointed his limits that he cannot pass, look away from him and leave him alone, that he may enjoy, like a hired hand, his day. For there is hope for a tree, if it be cut down, that it will sprout again, and that its shoots will not cease. Though its root grow old in the earth, and its stump die in the soil, yet at the scent of water it will bud and put out branches like a young plant.

Job 14:5-9 ESV

Be wise in the way you act toward outsiders; make the most of every opportunity. Let your conversation be always full of grace, seasoned with salt, so that you may know how to answer everyone.

Colossians 4:5-6 NIV

MAKING THE BEST
OF THE TIME WE HAVE

Our days may come to seventy years, or eighty,
if our strength endures; yet the best of them
are but trouble and sorrow, for they quickly
pass, and we fly away.

Psalm 90:10 NIV

My child, listen to me and do as I say, and you
will have a long, good life.

Proverbs 4:10 NLT

Now listen, you who say, "Today or tomorrow
we will go to this or that city, spend a year there,
carry on business and make money." Why, you
do not even know what will happen tomorrow.
What is your life? You are a mist that appears
for a little while and then vanishes. Instead, you
ought to say, "If it is the Lord's will, we will live
and do this or that."

James 4:13-15 NIV

The LORD keeps you from all harm and watches over your life. The LORD keeps watch over you as you come and go, both now and forever.

Psalm 121:7-8 NLT

Listen, I tell you a mystery: We will not all sleep, but we will all be changed – in a flash, in the twinkling of an eye, at the last trumpet.

1 Corinthians 15:51-52 NIV

Anyone who belongs to Christ has become a new person. The old life is gone; a new life has begun! And all of this is a gift from God, who brought us back to Himself through Christ.

2 Corinthians 5:17-18 NLT

MAKING THE BEST
OF THE TIME WE HAVE

LORD, make me to know my end, and what is the measure of my days, that I may know how frail I am. Indeed, You have made my days as handbreadths, and my age is as nothing before You; certainly every man at his best state is but vapor. Surely every man walks about like a shadow; surely they busy themselves in vain; he heaps up riches, and does not know who will gather them. And now, Lord, what do I wait for? My hope is in You.

Psalm 39:4-7 NKJV

You see me when I travel and when I rest at home. You know everything I do. You know what I am going to say even before I say it, LORD. You go before me and follow me. You place Your hand of blessing on my head.

Psalm 139:3-5 NLT

MAKING THE BEST
OF THE TIME WE HAVE

Whether you eat or drink or whatever you do,
do it all for the glory of God.

1 Corinthians 10:31 NIV

I concluded there is nothing better than to be
happy and enjoy ourselves as long as we can.
And people should eat and drink and enjoy
the fruits of their labor, for these are gifts from
God.

Ecclesiastes 3:12-13 NLT

For everything there is a season, and a time for
every matter under heaven: a time to be born,
and a time to die; a time to plant, and a time to
pluck up what is planted.

Ecclesiastes 3:1-2 ESV

MAKING THE BEST
OF THE TIME WE HAVE

We fix our eyes not on what is seen, but on what is unseen, since what is seen is temporary, but what is unseen is eternal.

2 Corinthians 4:18 NIV

God has made everything beautiful for its own time. He has planted eternity in the human heart, but even so, people cannot see the whole scope of God's work from beginning to end.

Ecclesiastes 3:11 NLT

Do not boast about tomorrow, for you do not know what a day may bring forth.

Proverbs 27:1 NKJV

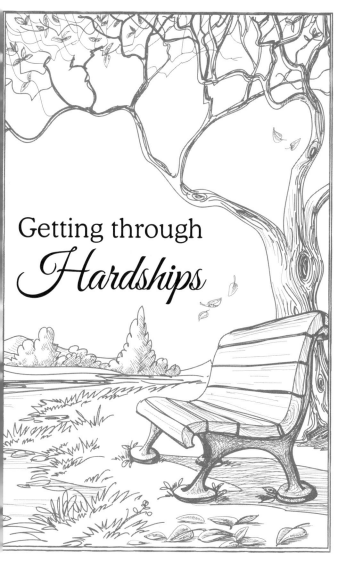

Getting through
Hardships

GETTING THROUGH HARDSHIPS

Blessed is the one who perseveres under trial because, having stood the test, that person will receive the crown of life.

James 1:12 NIV

We rejoice in our sufferings, knowing that suffering produces endurance, and endurance produces character, and character produces hope, and hope does not put us to shame, because God's love has been poured into our hearts through the Holy Spirit who has been given to us.

Romans 5:3-5 ESV

Since He Himself has gone through suffering and testing, He is able to help us when we are being tested.

Hebrews 2:18 NLT

Consider it pure joy, my brothers and sisters, whenever you face trials of many kinds, because you know that the testing of your faith develops perseverance. Let perseverance finish its work so that you may be mature and complete, not lacking anything.

James 1:2-4 NIV

The God of all grace, who called you to His eternal glory in Christ, after you have suffered a little while, will Himself restore you and make you strong, firm and steadfast.

1 Peter 5:10 NIV

I consider that the sufferings of this present time are not worth comparing with the glory that is to be revealed to us.

Romans 8:18 ESV

GETTING THROUGH HARDSHIPS

"In this world you will have trouble. But take heart! I have overcome the world."

John 16:33 NIV

He comforts us in all our troubles so that we can comfort others ... For the more we suffer for Christ, the more God will shower us with His comfort through Christ.

2 Corinthians 1:4-5 NLT

"I am the Lord your God who takes hold of your right hand and says to you,'Do not fear; I will help you.'"

Isaiah 41:13 NIV

GETTING THROUGH HARDSHIPS

As the elect of God, holy and beloved, put on tender mercies, kindness, humility, meekness, longsuffering.

Colossians 3:12 NKJV

Beloved, do not think it strange concerning the fiery trial which is to try you, as though some strange thing happened to you; but rejoice to the extent that you partake of Christ's sufferings, that when His glory is revealed, you may also be glad with exceeding joy.

1 Peter 4:12-13 NKJV

God had planned something better for us.

Hebrews 11:40 NIV

Those who suffer according to God's will should commit themselves to their faithful Creator and continue to do good.

1 Peter 4:19 NIV

"When you go through deep waters, I will be with you. When you go through rivers of difficulty, you will not drown. When you walk through the fire of oppression, you will not be burned up; the flames will not consume you."

Isaiah 43:2 NLT

If you suffer for doing good and you endure it, this is commendable before God.

1 Peter 2:20 NIV

I love the LORD because He hears my voice and my prayer for mercy. Because He bends down to listen, I will pray as long as I have breath! How kind the LORD is! How good He is! So merciful, this God of ours!

Psalm 116:1-2, 5 NLT

Be strong and do not give up, for your work will be rewarded.

2 Chronicles 15:7 NIV

The Lord knows how to rescue godly people from their trials.

2 Peter 2:9 NLT

Let us throw off everything that hinders and the sin that so easily entangles. And let us run with perseverance the race marked out for us.

Hebrews 12:1 NIV

"Don't let your hearts be troubled. Trust in God, and trust also in Me."

John 14:1 NLT

The LORD protects and preserves them – they are counted among the blessed in the land – He does not give them over to the desire of their foes. The LORD sustains them on their sickbed and restores them from their bed of illness.

Psalm 41:2-3 NIV

Path to
Peace

PATH TO PEACE

"I am leaving you with a gift – peace of mind and heart. And the peace I give is a gift the world cannot give. So don't be troubled or afraid."

John 14:27 NLT

"In Me you may have peace. In the world you will have tribulation; but be of good cheer, I have overcome the world."

John 16:33 NKJV

Jesus said, "Come to Me, all of you who are weary and carry heavy burdens, and I will give you rest."

Matthew 11:28 NLT

PATH TO PEACE

The mind governed by the Spirit is life and peace.

Romans 8:6 NIV

When a man's ways please the LORD, He makes even his enemies to be at peace with him.

Proverbs 16:7 NKJV

The LORD gives strength to His people;
the LORD blesses His people with peace.

Psalm 29:11 NIV

The peace of God, which surpasses all understanding, will guard your hearts and your minds in Christ Jesus.

Philippians 4:7 NKJV

Great peace have those who love Your law, and nothing can make them stumble.

Psalm 119:165 NIV

Let the peace of Christ rule in your hearts.

Colossians 3:15 ESV

You will keep in perfect peace those whose minds are steadfast, because they trust in You.

Isaiah 26:3 NIV

I will both lie down in peace, and sleep; for You alone, O LORD, make me dwell in safety.

Psalm 4:8 NKJV

PATH TO PEACE

Glory to God in the highest heaven, and on earth peace to those on whom His favor rests.

Luke 2:14 NIV

"Blessed are the peacemakers, for they shall be called sons of God."

Matthew 5:9 ESV

Submit to God and be at peace with Him; in this way prosperity will come to you.

Job 22:21 NIV

Because of God's tender mercy, the morning light from heaven is about to break upon us, to guide us to the path of peace.

Luke 1:78-79 NLT

PATH TO PEACE

God is not a God of confusion but of peace.

1 Corinthians 14:33 ESV

Those who are peacemakers will plant seeds of
peace and reap a harvest of righteousness.

James 3:18 NLT

The meek will inherit the land and enjoy peace
and prosperity.

Psalm 37:11 NIV

The work of righteousness will be peace,
and the effect of righteousness, quietness
and assurance forever.

Isaiah 32:17 NKJV

The God of peace be with you.

Romans 15:33 NIV

The kingdom of God is not a matter of eating and drinking but of righteousness and peace and joy in the Holy Spirit.

Romans 14:17 ESV

The Scriptures say, "If you want to enjoy life and see many happy days, keep your tongue from speaking evil and your lips from telling lies. Turn away from evil and do good. Search for peace, and work to maintain it."

1 Peter 3:10-11 NLT

Be completely humble and gentle; be patient, bearing with one another in love. Make every effort to keep the unity of the Spirit through the bond of peace.

Ephesians 4:2-3 NIV

Strive for peace with everyone, and for the holiness without which no one will see the Lord.

Hebrews 12:14 ESV

May God give you more and more mercy, peace, and love.

Jude 2 NLT

Forgiveness

in a Sinful World

FORGIVENESS IN A SINFUL WORLD

"I have blotted out, like a thick cloud, your transgressions, and like a cloud, your sins. Return to Me, for I have redeemed you."

Isaiah 44:22 NKJV

As high as the heavens are above the earth, so great is His love for those who fear Him; as far as the east is from the west, so far has He removed our transgressions from us.

Psalm 103:11-12 NIV

"I will forgive their wickedness, and I will never again remember their sins."

Hebrews 8:12 NLT

FORGIVENESS IN A SINFUL WORLD

"Though your sins are like scarlet, they shall be as white as snow; though they are red as crimson, they shall be like wool."

Isaiah 1:18 NIV

The Lord our God is merciful and forgiving.

Daniel 9:9 NLT

All the prophets testify about Him that everyone who believes in Him receives forgiveness of sins through His name.

Acts 10:43 NIV

You are a forgiving God, gracious and compassionate, slow to anger and abounding in love.

Nehemiah 9:17 NIV

FORGIVENESS IN A SINFUL WORLD

There is no condemnation for those who belong to Christ Jesus. And because you belong to Him, the power of the life-giving Spirit has freed you from the power of sin that leads to death.

Romans 8:1-2 NLT

If anyone sins, we have an Advocate with the Father, Jesus Christ the righteous. And He Himself is the propitiation for our sins, and not for ours only but also for the whole world.

1 John 2:1-2 NKJV

We praise God for the glorious grace He has poured out on us who belong to His dear Son. He is so rich in kindness and grace that He purchased our freedom with the blood of His Son and forgave our sins.

Ephesians 1:6-7 NLT

FORGIVENESS IN A SINFUL WORLD

Who is a God like You, who pardons sin and forgives the transgression of the remnant of His inheritance? You do not stay angry forever but delight to show mercy. You will again have compassion on us; You will tread our sins underfoot and hurl all our iniquities into the depths of the sea.

Micah 7:18-19 NIV

"Be encouraged, My child! Your sins are forgiven."

Matthew 9:2 NLT

It is the power of God that brings salvation to everyone who believes.

Romans 1:16 NIV

He has delivered us from the domain of darkness and transferred us to the kingdom of His beloved Son, in whom we have redemption, the forgiveness of sins.

Colossians 1:13-14 ESV

The LORD is my light and my salvation – whom shall I fear? The LORD is the stronghold of my life – of whom shall I be afraid?

Psalm 27:1 NIV

The LORD is the strength of His people, a fortress of salvation for His anointed one. Save Your people and bless Your inheritance; be their shepherd and carry them forever.

Psalm 28:8-9 NIV

FORGIVENESS IN A SINFUL WORLD

Christ was offered once for all time as a sacrifice to take away the sins of many people. He will come again, not to deal with our sins, but to bring salvation to all who are eagerly waiting for Him.

Hebrews 9:28 NLT

Everyone has sinned; we all fall short of God's glorious standard. Yet God freely and graciously declares that we are righteous. He did this through Christ Jesus when He freed us from the penalty for our sins. For God presented Jesus as the sacrifice for sin. People are made right with God when they believe that Jesus sacrificed His life, shedding His blood.

Romans 3:23-25 NLT

FORGIVENESS IN A SINFUL WORLD

He took a cup, and when He had given thanks He gave it to them, saying, "Drink of it, all of you, for this is My blood of the covenant, which is poured out for many for the forgiveness of sins."

Matthew 26:27-28 ESV

You were dead because of your sins and because your sinful nature was not yet cut away. Then God made you alive with Christ, for He forgave all our sins. He canceled the record of the charges against us and took it away by nailing it to the cross.

Colossians 2:13-14 NLT

If we confess our sins to Him, He is faithful and just to forgive us our sins and to cleanse us from all wickedness.

1 John 1:9 NLT

Trusting
the Lord

The LORD is good, a refuge in times of trouble. He cares for those who trust in Him.

Nahum 1:7 NIV

Trust in the LORD forever, for the LORD GOD is an everlasting rock. For He has humbled the inhabitants of the height, the lofty city.

Isaiah 26:4-5 ESV

May the God of hope fill you with all joy and peace as you trust in Him, so that you may overflow with hope by the power of the Holy Spirit.

Romans 15:13 NIV

TRUSTING THE LORD

It is better to take refuge in the LORD than to trust in people.

Psalm 118:8 ESV

"Do not let your hearts be troubled. You believe in God; believe also in Me."

John 14:1 NIV

Trust in Him at all times, you people; pour out your heart before Him; God is a refuge for us.

Psalm 62:8 NKJV

Blessed is the one who trusts in the LORD, whose confidence is in Him.

Jeremiah 17:7 NIV

TRUSTING THE LORD

Put your trust in the LORD.

Psalm 4:5 ESV

Some trust in chariots and some in horses,
but we trust in the name of the LORD our God.

Psalm 20:7 NIV

If we are faithful to the end, trusting God just
as firmly as when we first believed, we will
share in all that belongs to Christ.

Hebrews 3:14 NLT

"I will rescue those who love Me. I will protect
those who trust in My name."

Psalm 91:14 NLT

TRUSTING THE LORD

Let the morning bring me word of Your unfailing love, for I have put my trust in You. Show me the way I should go, for to You I entrust my life.

Psalm 143:8 NIV

Those who trust in the LORD will find new strength. They will soar high on wings like eagles. They will run and not grow weary. They will walk and not faint.

Isaiah 40:31 NLT

Many will see and fear the LORD and put their trust in Him. Blessed is the one who trusts in the LORD.

Psalm 40:3-4 NIV

TRUSTING THE LORD

It is with your heart that you believe and are justified, and it is with your mouth that you profess your faith and are saved. As Scripture says, "Anyone who believes in Him will never be put to shame."

Romans 10:10-11 NIV

Trust in the LORD with all your heart and lean not on your own understanding; in all your ways submit to Him, and He will make your paths straight.

Proverbs 3:5-6 NIV

Those who know Your name trust in You, for You, LORD, have never forsaken those who seek You.

Psalm 9:10 NIV

TRUSTING THE LORD

The fear of man brings a snare, but whoever trusts in the LORD shall be safe.

Proverbs 29:25 NKJV

Those who listen to instruction will prosper; those who trust the LORD will be joyful.

Proverbs 16:20 NLT

Trust in the LORD, and do good; dwell in the land, and feed on His faithfulness. Delight yourself also in the LORD, and He shall give you the desires of your heart.

Psalm 37:3-4 NKJV

TRUSTING THE LORD

The LORD is righteous in all His ways and faithful in all He does.

Psalm 145:17 NIV

He who dwells in the shelter of the Most High will abide in the shadow of the Almighty. I will say to the LORD, "My refuge and my fortress, my God, in whom I trust."

Psalm 91:1-2 ESV

I am trusting You, O LORD, saying, "You are my God!" My future is in Your hands.

Psalm 31:14-15 NLT

God Will Be *Good* to Us

Give thanks to the LORD, for He is good;
His love endures forever.

Psalm 107:1 NIV

The LORD is good to everyone. He showers
compassion on all His creation. All of Your
works will thank You, LORD, and Your faithful
followers will praise You.

Psalm 145:9-10 NLT

The LORD will guide you always; He will satisfy
your needs in a sun-scorched land and will
strengthen your frame. You will be like a
well-watered garden, like a spring whose
waters never fail.

Isaiah 58:11 NIV

Oh, taste and see that the LORD is good; blessed is the man who trusts in Him!

Psalm 34:8 NKJV

His divine power has given us everything we need for a godly life through our knowledge of Him who called us by His own glory and goodness. Through these He has given us His very great and precious promises.

2 Peter 1:3-4 NIV

"Why do you call Me good?" Jesus asked. "Only God is truly good."

Mark 10:18 NLT

You are good, and what You do is good; teach me Your decrees.

Psalm 119:68 NIV

Truly God is good to Israel, to such as are pure in heart.

Psalm 73:1 NKJV

For You, O Lord, are good and forgiving, abounding in steadfast love to all who call upon You.

Psalm 86:5 ESV

The earth is full of the goodness of the LORD.

Psalm 33:5 NKJV

Good and upright is the LORD; therefore He instructs sinners in His ways. He guides the humble in what is right and teaches them His way. All the ways of the LORD are loving and faithful toward those who keep the demands of His covenant.

Psalm 25:8-10 NIV

Every good gift and every perfect gift is from above, and comes down from the Father of lights, with whom there is no variation or shadow of turning.

James 1:17 NKJV

The LORD will do what is good in His sight.

2 Samuel 10:12 NIV

GOD WILL BE GOOD TO US

The LORD is good, a strong refuge when trouble comes. He is close to those who trust in Him.

Nahum 1:7 NLT

The LORD said, "I will cause all My goodness to pass in front of you, and I will proclaim My name, the LORD, in your presence. I will have mercy on whom I will have mercy, and I will have compassion on whom I will have compassion."

Exodus 33:19 NIV

The LORD God is a sun and shield; the LORD bestows favor and honor; no good thing does He withhold from those whose walk is blameless.

Psalm 84:11 NIV

GOD WILL BE GOOD TO US

Oh, how abundant is Your goodness, which You have stored up for those who fear You and worked for those who take refuge in You, in the sight of the children of mankind! In the cover of Your presence You hide them from the plots of men; You store them in Your shelter from the strife of tongues. Blessed be the LORD, for He has wondrously shown His steadfast love to me.

Psalm 31:19-21 ESV

We know that God causes everything to work together for the good of those who love God and are called according to His purpose for them. For God knew His people in advance, and He chose them to become like His Son, so that His Son would be the firstborn among many brothers and sisters.

Romans 8:28-29 NLT

GOD WILL BE GOOD TO US

Praise the LORD, for the LORD is good; sing to His name, for it is pleasant!

Psalm 135:3 ESV

In the past He permitted all the nations to go their own ways, but He never left them without evidence of Himself and His goodness. For instance, He sends you rain and good crops and gives you food and joyful hearts.

Acts 14:16-17 NLT

Give thanks to the LORD, for He is good! His faithful love endures forever.

Psalm 106:1 NLT

Seek
God Always

"Seek the Kingdom of God above all else, and live righteously, and He will give you everything you need."

Matthew 6:33 NLT

Let the hearts of those who seek the LORD rejoice! Seek the LORD and His strength; seek His presence continually! Remember the wondrous works that He has done, His miracles and the judgments He uttered. He is the LORD our God; His judgments are in all the earth.

1 Chronicles 16:10-12, 14 ESV

I seek You with all my heart; do not let me stray from Your commands.

Psalm 119:10 NIV

Let all those who seek You rejoice and be glad in You; let such as love Your salvation say continually, "The LORD be magnified!"

Psalm 40:16 NKJV

Submit yourselves therefore to God. Resist the devil, and he will flee from you. Draw near to God, and He will draw near to you.

James 4:7-8 ESV

Those who know Your name will put their trust in You; for You, LORD, have not forsaken those who seek You.

Psalm 9:10 NKJV

SEEK GOD ALWAYS

My heart says of You, "Seek His face!" Your face, LORD, I will seek. Do not hide Your face from me, do not turn Your servant away in anger; You have been my helper.

Psalm 27:8-9 NIV

Seek the LORD your God, and you will find Him if you seek Him with all your heart and with all your soul.

Deuteronomy 4:29 NKJV

"Ask, and it will be given to you; seek, and you will find; knock, and it will be opened to you. For everyone who asks receives, and the one who seeks finds, and to the one who knocks it will be opened."

Matthew 7:7-8 ESV

I love those who love me, and those who seek me diligently will find me.

Proverbs 8:17 NKJV

"Whoever believes in Me, as Scripture has said, rivers of living water will flow from within them." By this He meant the Spirit, whom those who believed in Him were later to receive.

John 7:38-39 NIV

Seek the LORD and His strength; seek His face evermore! Remember His marvelous works which He has done, His wonders, and the judgments of His mouth.

Psalm 105:4-5 NKJV

SEEK GOD ALWAYS

The LORD looks down from heaven on all mankind to see if there are any who understand, any who seek God.

Psalm 14:2 NIV

The LORD is with you while you are with Him. If you seek Him, He will be found by you, but if you forsake Him, He will forsake you.

2 Chronicles 15:2 ESV

The lions may grow weak and hungry, but those who seek the LORD lack no good thing.

Psalm 34:10 NIV

He made from one man every nation of mankind to live on all the face of the earth, having determined allotted periods and the boundaries of their dwelling place, that they should seek God, and perhaps feel their way toward Him and find Him. Yet He is actually not far from each one of us.

Acts 17:26-27 ESV

Devote your heart and soul to seeking the LORD your God.

1 Chronicles 22:19 NIV

If then you were raised with Christ, seek those things which are above, where Christ is, sitting at the right hand of God. Set your mind on things above, not on things on the earth.

Colossians 3:1-2 NKJV

SEEK GOD ALWAYS

You, God, are my God, earnestly I seek You; I thirst for You, my whole being longs for You, in a dry and parched land where there is no water.

Psalm 63:1 NIV

Seek the LORD while He may be found; call upon Him while He is near.

Isaiah 55:6 ESV

The LORD sees every heart and knows every plan and thought. If you seek Him, you will find Him. But if you forsake Him, He will reject you forever.

1 Chronicles 28:9 NLT

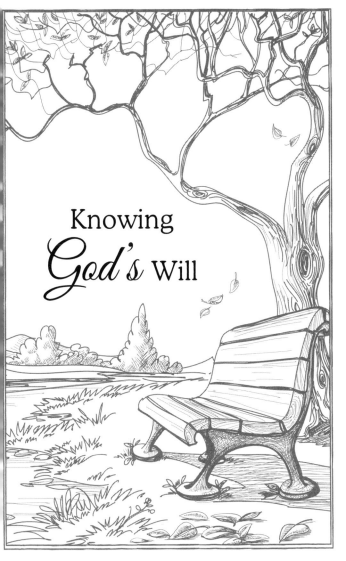

Knowing *God's* Will

KNOWING GOD'S WILL

Be thankful in all circumstances, for this is God's will for you who belong to Christ Jesus.

1 Thessalonians 5:18 NLT

Do not be conformed to this world, but be transformed by the renewal of your mind, that by testing you may discern what is the will of God, what is good and acceptable and perfect.

Romans 12:2 ESV

"I know the plans I have for you," declares the LORD, "plans to prosper you and not to harm you, plans to give you hope and a future. Then you will call on Me and come and pray to Me, and I will listen to you. You will seek Me and find Me when you seek Me with all your heart."

Jeremiah 29:11-13 NIV

"This is the only work God wants from you: Believe in the One He has sent."

John 6:29 NLT

For this is the will of God, that by doing good you should put to silence the ignorance of foolish people.

1 Peter 2:15 ESV

Be filled with the Holy Spirit, singing psalms and hymns and spiritual songs among yourselves, and making music to the Lord in your hearts. And give thanks for everything to God the Father in the name of our Lord Jesus Christ.

Ephesians 5:18-20 NLT

Do not be foolish, but understand what the will of the Lord is.

Ephesians 5:17 ESV

Continue to work out your salvation with fear and trembling, for it is God who works in you to will and to act in order to fulfill His good purpose. Do everything without grumbling or arguing, so that you may become blameless and pure, "children of God without fault in a warped and crooked generation." Then you will shine among them like stars in the sky as you hold firmly to the word of life.

Philippians 2:12-16 NIV

"Not everyone who says to Me, 'Lord, Lord,' shall enter the kingdom of heaven, but he who does the will of My Father in heaven."

Matthew 7:21 NKJV

God's will is for you to be holy, so stay away from all sexual sin. Then each of you will control his own body and live in holiness and honor.

1 Thessalonians 4:3-4 NLT

"I have come down from heaven to do the will of God who sent Me, not to do My own will. And this is the will of God, that I should not lose even one of all those He has given Me, but that I should raise them up at the last day. For it is My Father's will that all who see His Son and believe in Him should have eternal life."

John 6:38-40 NLT

Many are the plans in the mind of a man, but it is the purpose of the LORD that will stand.

Proverbs 19:21 ESV

The Father who knows all hearts knows what the Spirit is saying, for the Spirit pleads for us believers in harmony with God's own will.

Romans 8:27 NLT

Follow God's example, therefore, as dearly loved children and walk in the way of love, just as Christ loved us and gave Himself up for us as a fragrant offering and sacrifice to God.

Ephesians 5:1-2 NIV

You need to persevere so that when you have done the will of God, you will receive what He has promised.

Hebrews 10:35-36 NKJV

KNOWING GOD'S WILL

Do not love the world or the things in the world. If anyone loves the world, the love of the Father is not in him. For all that is in the world – the lust of the flesh, the lust of the eyes, and the pride of life – is not of the Father but is of the world. And the world is passing away, and the lust of it; but he who does the will of God abides forever.

1 John 2:15-17 NKJV

"What do you think? If a man has a hundred sheep, and one of them has gone astray, does he not leave the ninety-nine on the mountains and go in search of the one that went astray? And if he finds it, truly, I say to you, he rejoices over it more than over the ninety-nine that never went astray. So it is not the will of My Father who is in heaven that one of these little ones should perish."

Matthew 18:11-14 ESV

"Whoever does the will of God, he is My brother and sister and mother."

Mark 3:35 ESV

The Lord is not slack concerning His promise, as some count slackness, but is longsuffering toward us, not willing that any should perish but that all should come to repentance.

2 Peter 3:9 NKJV

He has shown you, O mortal, what is good. And what does the LORD require of you? To act justly and to love mercy and to walk humbly with your God.

Micah 6:8 NIV

The Root of
Happiness

This is the day that the LORD has made; let us rejoice and be glad in it.

Psalm 118:24 ESV

Those who sow with tears will reap with songs of joy.

Psalm 126:5 NIV

The LORD is my strength and song, and He has become my salvation.

Psalm 118:14 NKJV

Glory in His holy name; let the hearts of those who seek the LORD rejoice.

Psalm 105:3 NIV

"Rejoice because your names are written in heaven."

Luke 10:20 NKJV

"Be happy! Yes, leap for joy! For a great reward awaits you in heaven."

Luke 6:23 NLT

In Him our hearts rejoice, for we trust in His holy name.

Psalm 33:21 NIV

The joy of the LORD is your strength.

Nehemiah 8:10 NKJV

When Your words came, I ate them; they were my joy and my heart's delight.

Jeremiah 15:16 NIV

The LORD is my strength and shield. I trust Him with all my heart. He helps me, and my heart is filled with joy. I burst out in songs of thanksgiving.

Psalm 28:7 NLT

You turned my wailing into dancing; You removed my sackcloth and clothed me with joy, that my heart may sing Your praises and not be silent. LORD my God, I will praise You forever.

Psalm 30:11-12 NIV

THE ROOT OF HAPPINESS

Those who look to Him for help will be radiant with joy; no shadow of shame will darken their faces.

Psalm 34:5 NLT

Because You are my help, I sing in the shadow of Your wings.

Psalm 63:7 NIV

Many people say, "Who will show us better times?" Let Your face smile on us, Lord. You have given me greater joy than those who have abundant harvests of grain and new wine.

Psalm 4:6-7 NLT

THE ROOT OF HAPPINESS

The precepts of the LORD are right, giving joy to the heart. The commands of the LORD are radiant, giving light to the eyes. The fear of the LORD is pure, enduring forever. The decrees of the LORD are firm, and all of them are righteous.

Psalm 19:8-9 NIV

Honor and majesty are before Him; strength and gladness are in His place.

1 Chronicles 16:27 NKJV

The LORD your God will bless you in all your harvest and in all the work of your hands, and your joy will be complete.

Deuteronomy 16:15 NIV

THE ROOT OF HAPPINESS

Let all those who seek You rejoice and be glad in You; and let those who love Your salvation say continually, "Let God be magnified!"

Psalm 70:4 NKJV

For His anger lasts only a moment, but His favor lasts a lifetime; weeping may stay for the night, but rejoicing comes in the morning.

Psalm 30:5 NIV

Light shines on the godly, and joy on those whose hearts are right. May all who are godly rejoice in the LORD and praise His holy name!

Psalm 97:11-12 NLT

THE ROOT OF HAPPINESS

Our mouths were filled with laughter, our tongues with songs of joy. Then it was said among the nations, "The LORD has done great things for them." The LORD has done great things for us, and we are filled with joy.

Psalm 126:2-3 NIV

Shouts of joy and victory resound in the tents of the righteous: "The LORD's right hand has done mighty things!"

Psalm 118:15 NIV

Happy are the people whose God is the LORD!

Psalm 144:15 NKJV

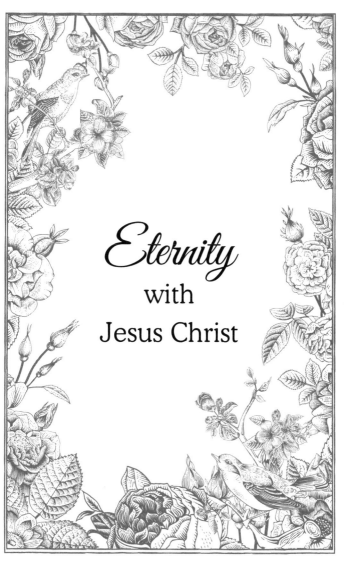

Eternity
with
Jesus Christ

"Truly, truly, I say to you, whoever believes has eternal life."

John 6:47 ESV

"Everyone who lives in Me and believes in Me will never ever die."

John 11:26 NLT

Whoever has the Son has life; whoever does not have the Son of God does not have life.

1 John 5:12 ESV

"My Father's will is that everyone who looks to the Son and believes in Him shall have eternal life."

John 6:40 NIV

ETERNITY WITH JESUS CHRIST

"God so loved the world that He gave His only begotten Son, that whoever believes in Him should not perish but have everlasting life."

John 3:16 NKJV

"Indeed, the time is coming when all the dead in their graves will hear the voice of God's Son, and they will rise again. Those who have done good will rise to experience eternal life, and those who have continued in evil will rise to experience judgment."

John 5:28-29 NLT

"I give them eternal life, and they shall never perish; no one will snatch them out of My hand. My Father, who has given them to Me, is greater than all; no one can snatch them out of My Father's hand. I and the Father are one."

John 10:28-30 NIV

ETERNITY WITH JESUS CHRIST

Therefore we do not lose heart. Even though our outward man is perishing, yet the inward man is being renewed day by day. For our light affliction, which is but for a moment, is working for us a far more exceeding and eternal weight of glory.

2 Corinthians 4:16-17 NKJV

I write these things to you who believe in the name of the Son of God so that you may know that you have eternal life.

1 John 5:13 NIV

For the wages of sin is death, but the free gift of God is eternal life through Christ Jesus our Lord.

Romans 6:23 NLT

ETERNITY WITH JESUS CHRIST

He who believes in the Son has everlasting life; and he who does not believe the Son shall not see life, but the wrath of God abides on him.

John 3:36 NKJV

"You can enter God's Kingdom only through the narrow gate. The highway to hell is broad, and its gate is wide for the many who choose that way. But the gateway to life is very narrow and the road is difficult, and only a few ever find it."

Matthew 7:13-14 NLT

"Do not work for the food that perishes, but for the food that endures to eternal life, which the Son of Man will give to you. For on Him God the Father has set His seal."

John 6:27 ESV

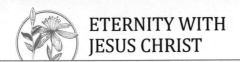

ETERNITY WITH JESUS CHRIST

Jesus answered and said to her, "Whoever drinks of this water will thirst again, but whoever drinks of the water that I shall give him will never thirst. But the water that I shall give him will become in him a fountain of water springing up into everlasting life."

John 4:13-14 NKJV

After Jesus said this, He looked toward heaven and prayed: "Father, the hour has come. Glorify Your Son, that Your Son may glorify You. For You granted Him authority over all people that He might give eternal life to all those You have given Him. Now this is eternal life: that they know You, the only true God, and Jesus Christ, whom You have sent."

John 17:1-3 NIV

ETERNITY WITH JESUS CHRIST

"If you refuse to take up your cross and follow Me, you are not worthy of being Mine. If you cling to your life, you will lose it; but if you give up your life for Me, you will find it."

Matthew 10:38-39 NLT

Do not be deceived: God is not mocked, for whatever one sows, that will he also reap. For the one who sows to his own flesh will from the flesh reap corruption, but the one who sows to the Spirit will from the Spirit reap eternal life.

Galatians 6:7-8 ESV

"Truly, truly, I say to you, whoever hears My word and believes Him who sent Me has eternal life. He does not come into judgment, but has passed from death to life."

John 5:24 ESV